I0158991

James Kay Publishing

Tulsa, Oklahoma

Being the Best Employee You Can Be!
ISBN 978-0-9850113-1-4

www.jameskaypublishing.com

e-mail: best@jameskaypublishing.com

For all of the employees, bosses, owners, trainers, managers, and associates I have had the privilege to work with in the past, present, and future.

Carolyn, thanks again for your second pair of eyes!

And as always - to my best friend, LaDonna - with all my love.

Before you read any further, here's the disclaimer:

Scan this code to order additional copies:

or visit:

http://www.jameskaypublishing.com/BookStore.html

Table of Contents

Introduction

Step Back and Think!

Evaluate Your Perspective

Do More than Expected

Recon Mission

The Tale of the Tape

The ol' Squeaky Wheel

Don't Throw Trash Around

Take the High Road

Train Your Replacement

Have a Servant's Attitude

Conclusion

"BE A YARDSTICK OF QUALITY.
SOME PEOPLE
AREN'T USED TO AN ENVIRONMENT
WHERE
EXCELLENCE IS EXPECTED." [i]

STEVE JOBS
(1955 - 2011)

AMERICAN INVENTOR & BUSINESSMAN

Introduction

It's a Hard Knock Life

It's a competitive world out there.

Dog-Eat-Dog.

Rat Race.

Ruthless comes to mind.

Everyone's "gunning" for you.

Stress levels are through the roof.

Upper management has changed again!

You feel unappreciated, overworked, and underpaid.

The last time you got an "attaboy" from the boss was... well, you can't remember the last time.

Or, maybe you work for a swell company. Everything is going swimmingly.

Productivity is up, morale is high, the next big bonus check just hit your mailbox.

You're a new hire.

You're an old-timer.

You're a rookie.

You're waiting to retire.

You're green behind the ears.

Just got a promotion.

Just got a demotion.

Just can't get a handle on things.

Can't stand the boss.

Can't keep up with technology.

Love the hours.

Love the overtime.

Get in line.

Many extremes, yes, but usually somewhere in the sea of job descriptions we find what folks call the "average employee."

You can still get in a rut, you can still be taken for granted, you can still wish you could clock out - if just for moment - to get your bearings or go to the Bahamas in your mind.

You may have opened this book because you do in fact want to BE THE BEST EMPLOYEE YOU CAN BE.

Someone may have given it to you because they thought you might want to improve in a few areas.

Maybe it's part of a new hire packet and you gotta read it before you get your name badge.

Whatever the case, we can always improve.

We don't, however, always have time to reinvent the wheel.

We can, however, do our best to make sure the wheel doesn't come off.

An article titled *"10 Things Your Boss Isn't Telling You"* listed some items a boss or manager wants to say to you but often won't.

- You talk too much at meetings
- You spend too much time on social media
- You're too emotional
- You dress inappropriately
- Your attitude stinks
- You have to be micromanaged
- You bring your personal life to work
- You don't play it straight
- You agree too much (don't offer differing opinions)[ii]

But, I'm assuming that if you're reading this, you have no plans to be *that* employee and fall in those traps noted above.

Is BECOMING THE BEST EMPLOYEE YOU CAN BE a guarantee of always keeping your job? No one can guarantee that. If they try, the next thing they'll do is attempt to sell you some real estate in the middle of the Brooklyn Bridge.

Now, while there's no guarantee of job security in today's world, BECOMING THE BEST EMPLOYEE YOU CAN BE can certainly skew things in your favor. But, it's going to require some honest assessment, evaluation, soul searching, and planning.

Who knows?

One day, you might be the employer.

Sometime you may go the route of self-employment and you'll be the only employee to carry the load.

Everything you do now to improve yourself will pay dividends down the road.

Ready to BE THE BEST EMPLOYEE YOU CAN BE?

Let's get started.

*"**A** JOURNEY OF A THOUSAND MILES
BEGINS WITH A SINGLE STEP."*[iii]

LAO-TZU

(604 BC - 531 BC)

CHINESE PHILOSOPHER

1
Step Back and Think!

first step
Taking the

Deciding to BE THE BEST EMPLOYEE YOU CAN BE is a conscious decision.

No one else can do it for you.

Your employer might wish you were the best at everything you do (and then wish they could clone you ten times.)

But, when we get to the bottom line, it's ultimately up to one person:

<u>YOU</u>

A recent Gallup Poll asked American workers to rate their satisfaction with 13 different aspects of their jobs, and the results show workers are most satisfied about their relationships with their coworkers and the physical safety conditions at their workplaces. Workers are least satisfied with the amount of on-the-job stress, the retirement benefits their employers offer, and their pay. One of the biggest changes over time has been the increased level of satisfaction with flexibility of work arrangements on the job. Satisfaction with job-related stress has also improved. Employees express higher satisfaction this year with their bosses or supervisors, the safety conditions at work, and coworker relations. In terms of how they feel about their jobs overall, just under half of workers say they are completely satisfied, with most of the rest "somewhat" satisfied; only 6% are dissatisfied.[iv]

Pros & Cons: Your personal inventory

Dynamics of the workplace.

dy·nam·ics (n) 1. change-producing forces: the forces that tend to produce activity and change in any situation or sphere of existence. 2. the relationships of power between the people in a group.

Take a moment to consider the interactions between you and others.

    You ⇔ Your Coworker
    You ⇔ The Customer
    You ⇔ The Supplier
    You ⇔ Your Immediate Supervisor
    You ⇔ Other (Human Resources, etc.)

The way you interact with others depends on, well it depends on who those others are. Your daily relationships are different, your history with each other is different, your responsibilities and accountabilities to them are different.

The constant is you.

So, before you can figure out how to interact productively and professionally with others, you first need to figure out who you (the constant) are.

Now, this isn't something you can do in one sitting. It's an ongoing, adaptive process. By assessing who you are, knowing what your capabilities, resources, background, and goals are, you can begin to get a handle on just how others might see you.

Your relationships can improve.

Your communications can improve.

Your day might just go a whole lot better.

And that's a good thing all around.

Set your eye on the prize

Set some goals.

Tangible goals.

Don't, as they say, try to eat the elephant in one bite.

Break it down.

Where do you want to be 6 months from now?

1 year?

5 years?

10 years?

At retirement?

To BE THE BEST EMPLOYEE YOU CAN BE, you've got to be heading in that direction.

Write down what you think it'll take. There are some nifty "My Road Map" pages near the end of this book for your convenience. It's a clean slate and you are certainly not limited to those pages. Take advantage of the open possibilities they offer. Go back often and review these thoughts as you continue to read. Add new ideas, reevaluate old ones, tweak, erase, group, highlight, categorize, list, whatever it takes - this is a work in progress.

You are a work in progress.

You always will be.

Ready to move to the next chapter?

Bring your goals with you and read on.

"You can't teach common sense."

Jim Bullard
(1935-1996)

Oilfield Worker & Dad

2

Evaluate Your Perspective

You are <u>selling</u> your time...

...but they don't have to buy it!

In a consumer-based economy there are two categories of folks. Those who sell and those who buy.

You're selling time.

They're buying time.

In order for that to equal out, you've got to put in a honest day's work for an honest day's pay. What a concept!

The Law of Supply states that at higher prices, producers are willing to offer more products for sale than at lower prices.

The Law of Supply states that the supply increases as prices increase and decreases as prices decrease.

The Law of Supply states that those already in business will try to increase productions as a way of increasing profits.

The Law of Demand states that people will buy more of a product at a lower price than at a higher price, if nothing changes.

The Law of Demand states that at a lower price, more people can afford to buy more goods and more of an item more frequently, than they can at a higher price.

The Law of Demand states that at lower prices, people tend to buy some goods as a substitute for others more expensive.[v]

What kind of value
are they getting?

Consider these two chunks of information:

I think there is some physical limit to the amount of work that you can get done in the day and beyond that, if you try to get people to do more of it, your productivity drops off so much that you're getting almost nothing from it.[vi]

Are workers really expected to work 8 hours per day, non-stop? According to a Salary.com follow-up survey of Human Resource managers, companies assume that employees will waste 0.94 hours per day. They take this into account when they do their compensation planning. However, those managers privately suspect that employees waste 1.6 hours per day. In fact, employees admit to wasting 2.09 hours per day.[vii]

Are you constantly making or taking personal calls? Doing something non-business related on your cell phone? Texting? Tweeting?

How about playing games on your computer, browsing the internet for personal items, social chat rooms, e-mails?

Constantly heading for the door to take a smoke break? Some folks seem to be so addicted to cigarettes that they have to take a smoke break from their smoke break. I've had many conversations with smokers about how difficult it is to quit. Yes, it is an addiction. Yes, it is a crutch. Yes, it calms your nerves. But, do you think your employer really wants to pay you to do it?

"I'm on a break," you reason. "It's my time."

Perhaps.

Consider how valuable your time is. There are only so many hours in the day. Subtract the time you sleep, you eat, you commute, you work, etc. There's actually very little "me" time left in the day. Put a value on it. Do a little math. That "me" time is really, really valuable. And you give it up to a little stick of flaming tobacco. You let it dictate to you that you're going to risk your health. You are going to stand out in the rain or the freezing north wind. You're going to stand next to that stinky smoke hole one more time. That little stick of flaming tobacco does not own you...or does it?

Take back <u>your</u> time and it might just add up to a few more years with the grandkids. Something to think about.

(If you want to go throw that pack in the garbage, go ahead. I'll put away my soap box and we'll meet back here.)

What about just plain goofing off?

There are lots of ways to do anything but work. Texting, playing games on the computer, staring out the window, wondering off the premises, personal phone calls, visiting with other workers - It still all amounts to the same thing.

The Flip Side of the Coin

Back in my younger days, I worked in a mechanic shop. Everyday around midmorning, the order would go in for who wanted hotlinks and chips. Then someone (sometimes me) would gather all the money and head down to the quick stop to fill the orders.

Now, when this ritual began, folks would voice their preferences, shell out the cash, and go back to work until the snacks arrived. (By the way, these were some of the best hotlinks I've ever had, before or since. But I digress.)

Over the course of the summer, a raggedy bench seat from a wrecked truck appeared next to the wall near the mechanic's ol' gunmetal gray desk. Guys would grab a cup of coffee or a soda from the pop box and sit and wait for the food to arrive. Salty stories were swapped and unbelievable tales were told. Then other chairs of all types began to join the circle. Soon there was quite a crowd. The break just seemed to get longer and more populated.

Eventually the "big boss" had had enough. He commandeered me to go to the dime store to buy poster board and markers. When I returned, he handed me a slip of paper and told me to put what he had written on the sign and nail it to the wall over the old truck bench. It read...

LOAFER'S SHACK
↓ LOAFERS ASSEMBLE HERE ↓

Everybody got the message and the breaks went back to the old routine. (I visited the shop a few years later and the sign was still there!)

Be aware of the little things that can eventually grow into large things. Don't get to the point where the "big boss" puts a loafer sign over your head.

Now, am I saying that you have to hold your nose to the grindstone every second of every minute you're at work? Certainly not. Let's don't swing the pendulum to the other extreme. Just be aware of your time and what you are doing with it. A conversation with a co-worker might start off work related, but it's easy to get off track. Keep yourself accountable.

Top Time-Wasting Activities (%)

1. Surfing Internet (personal use) 44.7%
2. Socializing with co-workers 23.4%
3. Conducting personal business 6.8%
4. Spacing out 3.9%
5. Running errands off-premises 3.1%
6. Making personal phone calls 2.3%
7. Applying for other jobs 1.3%
8. Planning personal events 1.0%
9. Arriving late / Leaving early 1.0%
10. Other 12.5%[viii]

Would you employ you?

> I once walked up to the counter of a chain taco restaurant to order a meal and the cashier was wearing a spiked dog collar.
>
> My comment to him was, "I'm guessing your District Manager doesn't drop by very often."

Turn the tables and put the shoe on the other foot.

Let's say (for illustration purposes) you're elected "King for a Day" in the Land of Human Resources. You get to be the "Big Boss" today. For 24 hours you make all the decisions.

First order of business. Do you keep yourself as an employee? Sure there might be a couple of other guys you would show the door.

Based on your honest assessment, would you keep you?

Just something to think about...

"Once you stop learning,
you start dying." [ix]

Albert Einstein
(1879 -1955)

Theoretical Physicist
& Really Smart Guy

3
Do More than Expected

Kick these two words to the curb

IMPOSSIBLE   **CAN'T**

Don't use 'em.

Don't say 'em.

Don't think 'em.

Never stop learning

Some folks try to learn a new word every day.

Others work crossword puzzles, or watch Jeopardy, or read a newspaper, or...

Learning doesn't necessarily involve going back to school.

You can pick up new information and knowledge from all around you.

The key is this: First you must want to expand your horizons. Everything else will fall into place after that.

Ask questions.

Investigate further.

Dig deeper.

Don't always take things at face value.

Books, magazines, web-sites, company literature, brochures, blogs, newsletters - be on the lookout for anything relating to your job, your company, your customers.

Follow-up. Follow-up. Follow-up.

Someone once said that the three most important things in real estate are: location, location, location.

Why?

Because it's very hard to sell a building to someone who wants to open a restaurant if there aren't any people nearby to come in for a meal.

This ain't rocket surgery.

The same holds true when you strive to do more than what is expected of you.

- When you follow-up,
  you show interest.

- When you follow-up,
  you show you care.

- When you follow-up,
  you show that you
  are concerned with
  the bigger picture.

"But," you say, "I just work on an assembly line. I put Tab A into Slot B and pass it on down the line. Same 'ol - Same 'ol. Day in and day out."

Or you say, "Stocking shelves doesn't require any follow-up. I stick to the plan-o-gram and put everything where they say to put it."

How about:

"I just wash cars."

-or-

"I just ring the sales."

-or-

"I just drive...

teach...

draw...

clerk...

type...

push a broom..."

You fill in the blank.

No matter what you do, no matter what your assignment, task, or duty - there is something you can follow-up on.

How did the finished product perform?

Was the sales letter successful?

Did the customer like what they purchased?

Look at this through the lens of what you do.

Consider how follow-up will make you a better employee.

- By helping you understand what an important part you play in the overall scheme of things.
- By showing others that you take enough pride in your work to be concerned about the outcome.
- By learning new facets of the overall job, so that when the time comes for evaluation and promotion you have a whole lot more knowledge than the other guy.

See? There are dividends to not only you, but your employer, and their customers and clients.

Win-win situations are nice.
Win-win-win situations get you noticed.

"WHAT ONE MAN CAN DO,
ANOTHER CAN DO." [x]

Charles Morse

ENTREPRENEUR & SURVIVALIST
"THE EDGE" (1997)

4
Recon Mission

Keep your ears open

Listen.

Two ears and one mouth.

There's a reason.

Find out what the need is and fill that need.

Sometimes opportunity doesn't knock very loud. Sometimes you gotta listen for it. You've got to be paying attention.

"Boy, I wish somebody would just..."

"Wouldn't it be great if..."

"Somebody ought to..."

"They're looking for someone to..."

"Something just opened up in..."

"Can you believe it? The customer asked for..."

Keep your eyes peeled

Look.

Keep up with what's posted on the bulletin boards.

Read the company newsletter.

Read trade magazines.

Pay attention to memos.

Safety signs aren't just for decoration.

Be aware of your surroundings. What's there? What's missing? What can be improved? What can be made safer? What can be simplified? What is redundant?

Pay attention to your fellow employees. Are they struggling with something you can help with? Are you aware of some new procedure they might have missed? Do they feel part of the team?

There's no such thing as a...

...dumb question.

Yeah, I know you know that.

Ask questions.

Seek clarification.

Communication is a two-way street.

It shows you care enough to do your job right.

"I CAN ACCEPT FAILURE,
EVERYONE FAILS AT SOMETHING.
BUT I CAN'T ACCEPT NOT TRYING." [xi]

MICHAEL Jordon
(1963 -   )

FORMER
AMERICAN PROFESSIONAL
BASKETBALL PLAYER
& ACTIVE BUSINESSMAN

5
The Tale of the Tape

What are your standards?

Ever hear of a benchmark?

A benchmark is something which sets the standard against which others are measured.

They use it when surveying land when a new house is built. If the benchmark is off, guess what? The house will be off too. Maybe sitting crooked on the lot, or over the property line - you get the idea.

Where's your personal benchmark?

Do you even know if you have one?

Let's see if we can find it.

Think about the language you use around others. Does your vocabulary consist of about six words and five of them aren't printable here, and two would make a sailor blush?

Think about how you treat others.

Think about your ethics.

Think about what you place value on.

Think about how others perceive you.

If you're not too proud of some of these answers, your benchmark might figuratively be down at the city dump.

Am I stepping on toes here?

Good.

Pick a new benchmark. Measure yourself against it. Watch your language. It might seem okay around the locker room or the break table to use foul language, but it's really not. You're more creative than that. Foul language can really limit just how far you can go.

Expand your vocabulary. Go back and review "Never stop learning" in Chapter 3.

How do you treat others? Do you talk down to them? Never listen to their opinion? Don't value them as a human being? Maybe "just a little" harmless harassment?

Harassment is not an option. Sexual, verbal, emotional, physical. It does not build you up. It does not give you more power. It does not bode well for your continued employment.

Don't go there.

Set your benchmark in good solid ground.

Who knows? Perhaps others in the future will set their benchmark on you.

How to be perfekct perfect

If you think you are - go back and take another crack at that self assessment.

I once ran for Senior Class Vice President on this campaign slogan:

Genius at Work:
Mistakes Made While You Wait

Successful? Let's just say that from now until the end of this book, you can refer to me as "Mr. Vice President."

No, not really.

Unless you feel you must.

Learn from your mistakes. Count on there being a few every now and again. Pick yourself up and dust yourself off. Learn to bounce. Evaluate what went wrong and go for a better outcome.

Is it okay if you don't get the credit?

"But, it was my idea!"

Others will take credit for what you did. Or, diminish your contribution. Or, steal all of your thunder.

Yeah, it happens sometimes.

You're bigger than that.

Sometimes you have to see the overall picture and be a team player. Take one for the team, as they say. Of course it hurts. Rub some dirt on it.

Let them run all over you?

Didn't say that.

Be smart.

There are often channels you can go through to get what you are due. Make notes, track dates, and keep a level head. Make your case calmly and with certainty. Yelling, pointing fingers, and sowing discord will take you down the wrong road. Know your rights. If you have a legitimate case to make and nobody is listening, then explore your options. But, keep your cool.

Now, with that being said, let's consider the case of the "squeaky wheel."

HATE TO BE A KICKER,

I ALWAYS LONG FOR PEACE,

BUT THE WHEEL THAT DOES THE SQUEAKING

IS THE ONE THAT GETS THE GREASE."[xii]

Attributed to

JOSH Billings

(1818 - 1885)

AMERICAN HUMORIST

6
The ol' Squeaky Wheel

Squeaky ain't always bad

Problems arise.

Important things are overlooked.

Procedures aren't followed.

But, it might be like that defective tail light on your car - If someone doesn't point it out to you, how are you ever going to know about it?

Be a squeaky wheel in a good way.

Be ready with solutions before you present the problem.

"Somebody oughta fix that thing before somebody gets hurt," you say in passing, but don't properly report it. Then somebody does get hurt, maybe even you. How are you going to feel then?

It's all about taking responsibility. Don't depend on the other guy.

Ever been in a store and see someone rip into a box to see the product inside before they buy it? I mean really rip apart the packaging? What do they usually do?

Put it back in the box and take it to the cashier for purchase?

No.

They take the one behind it, in the nice box, even if they plan to open it as soon as they get home. What does that teach the kid sitting in the shopping cart watching them?

Responsibility?

No, of course not.

To BE THE BEST EMPLOYEE YOU CAN BE, you've got to be responsible, exemplify responsibility, and expect others to be responsible as well.

The Shadow knows

A bad rep

Do you know someone who is a constant complainer? Nothing ever satisfies them. In their opinion, you can't do anything right.

How about someone who cries "wolf"? Someone who can perceive a problem miles over the horizon? It's all doom and gloom with them. The sky is falling. Paranoia with every assignment. Better to do nothing at all than to fail.

Then there's "the whiner." It's too hard. It's too heavy. I didn't sign on for this. It's not in my contract. Let them do it. It's their problem.

Or how about the "tattle-tale"?

Sound childish?

It is.

Step back and make sure it's not you.

One thing you do not want, if you aspire to BE THE BEST EMPLOYEE YOU CAN BE, is a bad reputation.

If you are constantly complaining, grouching, whining, telling on someone, or dispelling doom and gloom all of the time, eventually no one is going to listen to you.

Why should they? If you never offer a solution. Never see the glass half full. Never take responsibility for your own actions.

There's that word again:
→ **Responsibility**.

The Rat Patrol

There was a television show back in the 1960's about four guys in two Jeeps that drove all over the deserts of North Africa in World War II trying to disrupt the enemy. Called themselves the "Rat Patrol."

Boy, were they ever a squeaky wheel!

But, every week they were successful in their mission.

So, how did less than a handful of men take on a whole enemy regiment under such terrible conditions?

Simple.

They picked battles they could win.

There will be times you have something you should complain about or bring to someone's attention. Not saying not to do that.   But, as noted in the previous section, if you get a bad rep they might not listen to you.

Weigh it out.

Again. Be smart. Pick battles you can win. Sometimes you just gotta let things slide. If it's not a safety issue or someone is being dishonest or harassing, then think about whether this is the circumstance you want to take your stand on.   When it's important, it's important, but by thinking about choosing your battles wisely, you're forcing yourself to think things through to their logical and possible outcomes. You're evaluating the big, big difference between the *important* and the *trivial*.

"…WE SHALL MEET THE ENEMY,

AND NOT ONLY MAY HE BE OURS,

HE MAY BE US." [xiii]

WALT Kelly

(1913-1973)

AMERICAN ANIMATOR & CARTOONIST
BEST KNOWN FOR THE COMIC STRIP, POGO

7
Don't Throw Trash Around

From the outside looking in

You want to work for the best employer you can.

Don't you?

So, can you think of someone who might make them look bad In the eyes of the customer, potential future employees, and the public in general?

Is that person holding this book right now?

Maybe you don't work on the front lines. You might be behind the scenes. But, be aware that what you do has a ripple effect.

If you're dissatisfied with your employer or company and take that out into the world...

...maybe at the dinner table.

...maybe at the place you get your hair cut.

...or on the bowling team.

...the grocery store, gym, post office, to the delivery man, the vendor, the guy who brings the donuts...

You are doing both yourself and your employer a disservice. Keep your business - your business. Take care of it "in house" as they say. In other words, don't air your dirty laundry in public.

Reflections

Who makes them look good? You do.

Why?

Because you are striving to BE THE BEST EMPLOYEE YOU CAN BE!

You are a reflection of them and they are a reflection of you.

Take some pride in where you work. If it's not a place you can take pride in, then you be the one to make the conscience decision to make it so.

Ferris Wheel keep on turnin'

Newton's third law states:

FOR EVERY ACTION,
THERE IS AN
EQUAL
AND
OPPOSITE REACTION

Whoa! That's some kind of physics thing, isn't it?

Maybe so, but you can apply it to your actions at work. Every action you take and every choice you make will have a consequence.

Some good.

Some bad.

Some may be beyond your control, but for those which are - you need to make a conscious decision to go for the favorable outcome.

In what you say.
In your attitude.
In your work ethic.
In... you get the point.

Let's just keep it simple.

From physics to farming.
Think about it this way.
You reap what you sow.

"I WOULD CITE REGULATION,
BUT I KNOW YOU WILL SIMPLY
IGNORE IT." [xiv]

SPOCK
(2230 - 2285/2286 - ?)

SCIENCE OFFICER
& AMBASSADOR AT LARGE
"STAR TREK" (2009)

8
Take the High Road

You or that other guy

Remember when you were young and you wanted to do something an adult thought you ought not to do? You probably resorted to some of that "kid logic" and said something like, "But, the other kids are doing it!"

What reply did you get?

Come on, admit it.

"Well, if the other kids jumped off a cliff, would you jump off too?"

Doh!

Thwarted again.

But, of course we never admitted it.

It still applies today just as much as it did then. Just because the other employees are doing it, if it's wrong - it's wrong.

Who's going to step up and be the leader here?

That other guy leading you down the path and off the cliff?

Or you?

Setting the good example, no matter how difficult the peer pressure might get.

Focus on Honesty.

Focus on Integrity.

Focus on Morals.

Focus on Example.

And what's that spell? H.I.M.E. Which is not a real word and makes a lousy mnemonic device.

But, you're not focusing on that.

You're focusing on Honesty, Integrity, Morals, and Example.

You just never know who might be...

...watching.

Yes, someone is watching.

They notice.

That's not paranoia.

If they're running their business well and have a sense of responsibility to their owners, customers, stockholders, and yes, even you, then it's just a fact of employment life.

Speaking of responsibility. It seems to keep cropping up now and again, doesn't it?

re·spon·si·bil·I·ty (n)   1. the state, fact, or position of being accountable to somebody or for something.

Take responsibility for your actions.

This means you.

Man up

Let's talk a bit about constructive criticism.

Giving and Getting.

Giving is the easy one of the two, so about getting...

What's the first thing people do when someone gives them criticism?

They go all defensive. Shields up. Prepare to repel boarders.

Why?

Because most criticism is perceived as negative. The old adage - *If you can't say something good about someone, then don't say anything at all -* is not generally the rule of the land.

I once had an assistant manager go all ballistic on me when I told him a corrective interview was going into his file. My mistake. Forgot to forewarn him that a corrective interview at this particular company could be either positive or negative. He'd done an outstanding job and I wanted to commend him for it and have that commendation placed in his permanent file. The last place he'd worked, they used corrective interviews to quickly put an employee on the fast track to the unemployment line.

So, the next time someone offers you some criticism, take a deep breath, count to ten, and listen to see if it's constructive or destructive. Don't take it personal, even though it's easy to do. The goal should be for a great end result: you as a better employee.

The converse is true when giving constructive criticism. Don't get personal. Stick to the facts. Be clear. It might take time. It might take clarification. You might have to face defense and resistance. Stop talking and listen. Same goal as above - a great end result. You'll be a better employee and they will too.

"AND SERGEANT HULKA ISN'T ALWAYS GONNA BE HERE TO BE THAT BIG TOE FOR US." [xv]

JOHN WINGER

ARMY MISFIT
"STRIPES" (1981)

9
Train Your Replacement

One engine, many cars

Why would you want to train your own replacement? Doesn't that go against the survival instinct? Work-wise that is. If you teach someone how to do your job as well as you do, isn't there the possibility that they may very well take over your job and nudge you out the door?

Unfortunately in today's business culture, it does seem that wisdom and skill aren't a lock. Companies count the beans and figure if they can pay someone fewer beans than you to do the same job, then bottom line that's the best thing to do. That's why they call it 'Human' Resources.

That's short term thinking.

The best employees don't think short term.

Our goal here is to help you BECOME THE BEST EMPLOYEE YOU CAN BE.

So, let's don't think short term.

Let's think long term.

Bean counters, are you paying attention?

To BE THE BEST EMPLOYEE YOU CAN BE, you need to consider your role as a leader.

That doesn't necessarily mean the "rah, rah" guy out front.

A leader can be influential in a lot of different ways. Through example. Through encouragement. Through caring that others are successful also.

> Be training others to do your work. It is no compliment to anyone's effectiveness and leadership for any work to show a decline after he or she moves, is promoted, or retires.[xvi]

Not everyone can be the engine. Some have to be the cars. But those cars all contribute to the whole train. If one doesn't do its job, it drags down the ones in front and hinders the ones behind.

By training your replacement, you add to the overall quality of the whole.

And, believe it or not, you add to your own quality as well.

How?

When you teach or train someone else, you hone your own skills and knowledge.

It makes you think.

You have to break things down into steps, components, and sequences.

As you do this, you have the opportunity to analyze the smaller things which make up the whole. You discover even better and more efficient ways of doing things. You come up with better ideas.

You move up and who takes your place? Yep, it's that better trained person.

And you are both better organized. More confident. More proficient. More capable.

Keeping it on the track

What usually happens when you have to be away because of sickness, family emergencies, or vacation?

In the case of vacation, you often have time to bring someone up to speed on what they need to do to cover your work while you're away. You can go over with them in person where things are, how things work, etc.

When you're suddenly out sick or have to be away because of an unforeseen event, that can be another matter.

Your fill-in doesn't know the job well enough to do it properly.

They're not familiar with your filing system.

They can't find the keys.

So, what do they do?

A) Bluff their way through it.
B) Do as little as possible until you get back.
C) Make a royal mess of things.

-or-

D) Keep the train on track so that when you return, it's as if you never left. Things continue in a normal fashion and all is well in the world.

The light at the end of the tunnel

You really don't expect that fourth answer do you? You should, and you can, if you think seriously about the benefits of training your own replacement.

"...Well Done,
Good and faithful servant..." [xvii]

Matthew 25:21

10
Have a Servant's Attitude

What's in it for you?

If you're asking, "What's in it for me?" take a minute to contemplate two words up there above the line:

Servant

Attitude

When you put others before yourself, you are way ahead of a good majority of the population. If you don't sit down and really think about what those two words mean you can work yourself into a quirky paradigm that goes something like this:

"I'll have a Servant's Attitude and serve others, therefore since I'm doing something good for someone else, it will come around that something good will happen to me."

Do you see how that thinking shifts you out of a Servant's Attitude?

With a Servant's Attitude you take yourself out of the equation on the other side of the equal sign. You keep yourself on this side of it. You do things because they are the *right* thing to do, regardless of the outcome in relation to you. Sometimes, you might get something residually positive. Other times you won't. Don't worry about it. You can't take gravy to the grave. He who dies with the most toys does not win.

What's in it for them?

Everything.

What's in it for everyone?

A Servant's Attitude goes against the way society thinks.

They will try to take advantage of you, push you aside, steal your thunder, grab your glory, and step on your toes.

The "world out there" just doesn't get it. They won't give you credit, they won't offer you a hand, they won't give you a boost, they won't point you out.

But, there are some...

...who will.

"OF ALL THE THINGS YOU WEAR,

YOUR EXPRESSION

IS THE MOST IMPORTANT." [xviii]

Janet Lane

(? -)

AUTHOR

BONUS
<u>What a difference this can make!</u>

Smile.

Do it often.
Do it consistently.
It's just that simple.
You'll be amazed at the instant results.

*"**B**E THE CHANGE*

YOU WANT TO SEE

IN THE WORLD" [xix]

Mahatma Gandhi

(1869 - 1948)

INDIAN **P**HILOSOPHER

Conclusion

Putting it all together

Okay, so we've reached the end of this thing. Now, you're on your own. Here's a quick review.

It's really all about fundamentals. Getting back to basics. Taking responsibility. The A B C's of doing your job right, doing it well, doing it with integrity, and doing it with an attitude that at the end of the day gives you a reason to get up tomorrow morning and do it all over again...

...with a profoundly deep sense of accomplishment and purpose.

"THERE ARE NO CONSTRAINTS
ON THE HUMAN MIND,
NO WALLS AROUND THE HUMAN SPIRIT,
NO BARRIERS TO OUR PROGRESS
EXCEPT THOSE WE OURSELVES ERECT." xx

Ronald Reagan
(1911 - 2004)

AMERICAN PRESIDENT

About The Author

With over three decades of training and writing experience, Derek Bullard stays busy on many projects.

He holds a degree in Business Administration from The University of Oklahoma and has worked with numerous companies and foundations, both large and small. He has many years of experience in employment training, sales, management, marketing, supervision, and administration. Derek has been named "Employee of the Month", "Employee of the Year", and "Best of the Best" - each from a different employer.

Over the years, he's published both fiction and non-fiction in national and international publications, garnered numerous writing awards, as well as being a Contributing Editor for a national business publication. His novels, *MAYAN MOON* and *TWICE IN A BLUE MOON*, are available from James Kay Publishing and are also on *Kindle* and *Nook*.

MY ROAD MAP

MY ROAD MAP

MY ROAD MAP

ENDNOTES

[i] http://www.brainyquote.com/quotes/keywords/excellence.
html, (accessed October 8, 2011)

[ii] Alison Green, "10 Things Your Boss Isn't Telling You"
U.S. News & World Report, May 12, 2011,
(accessed October 5, 2011)

[iii] http://www.quotationspage.com/search.php3?homesearch
=LAO-TZU&page=2, (accessed October 5, 2011)

[iv] Joseph, Carroll, "U.S. Workers Remain Largely Satisfied With
Their Jobs", Gallup November 27, 2007
http://www.gallup.com/poll/102898/US-Workers-Remain-
Largely-Satisfied-Their-Jobs.aspx, (accessed October 8, 2011)

[v] http://www.curriculumlink.org/econ/materials/sdlaws.
html, (accessed October 10, 2011)

[vi] Peter Cappelli, (Wharton Business School, University of
Pennsylvania), *NPR*, August 8, 2007
http://www.npr.org/templates/story/story.php?storyId=
12418102, (accessed October 8, 2011)

[vii] Don Malachowski, "Wasted Time at Work Costing
Companies Billions" *SFGate,* July 11, 2005
http://www.sfgate.com/cgi-bin/article.cgi?f
=/g/a/2005/07/11/wastingtime.TMP,
(accessed October 8, 2011)

[viii] ibid

[ix] http://www.famous-quotes.net/Quote.aspx?Stop_
Learning_Start_Dying, (accessed October 5, 2011)

[x] http://www.imdb.com/title/tt0119051/quotes,
(accessed October 7, 2011)

[xi] http://www.brainyquote.com/quotes/authors/m/michael_
jordan.html, (accessed October 5, 2011)

[xii] http://www.quotecounterquote.com/search?q=Josh+billings,
(accessed October 5, 2011)

[xiii] http://www.igopogo.com/we_have_met.htm,
(accessed October 5, 2011)

[xiv] http://www.imdb.com/title/tt0796366/quotes,
(accessed October 5, 2011)

[xv] imdb.com http://www.imdb.com/title/tt0083131/quotes,
(accessed October 7, 2011)

[xvi] Jerrie Barbaer; via the weekly bulletin of the Harrisburg
church of Christ in Harrisburg, PA.

[xvii] *English Standard Version*

[xviii] http://www.goodreads.com/quotes/search?q=Janet+Lane
&commit=Search,
(accessed October 5, 2011)

[xix] http://thinkexist.com/quotation/be_the_change_you_want
_to_see_in_the_world/148490.html,
(accessed October 5, 2011)

[xx] http://www.brainyquote.com/quotes/authors/r/ronald_
reagan_4.html,
(accessed October 7, 2011)

www.ingramcontent.com/pod-product-compliance
Lightning Source LLC
Chambersburg PA
CBHW070524030426
42337CB00016B/2091